50

Inspirational Prayers for Financial Breakthrough and Divine Healing

D1304740

By Yolanda Washington-Cowan

Unless otherwise indicated, scriptures are taken from the King James Version (KJV).

50 Inspirational Prayers for Financial Breakthrough and Divine Healing

Copyright @ 2018
ISBN-13:978-0999777619
ISBN-10:0999777610

by Yolanda Washington-Cowan
All rights reserved
Published by
B-Inspired Publishing
7285 Winchester Road, Suite 109
Memphis, TN 38125
www.B-Inspiredpub.com
Printed in the United States
First Edition: March 2018

Table of Contents

ACKNOWLEDGEMENTS

A special thanks to my husband, Vaughn Cowan, my mother Delores and son Kenneth, Jr for their love, support, and encouragement.

Also to Phyllis McVay for editing and proofreading, and having patience in assisting me with this book.

INTRODUCTION

It is expedient we pray for the grace of God to sustain us in our fast-paced world that is full of lack, poverty, economic instability, and diseases. There is an urgent need for everyone who desires improvement in their finance and health to reconnect with God through scripture based prayers.

> *Delight yourself in the Lord, and he will give you the desires of your heart (Psalm 37:4)*

Therefore, this book contains a list of prayer points that have been compiled to guide you on how to commune with God, who is able to exceed your expectations.

> *Now unto him that is able to do exceeding abundantly above all that we ask or think, according to the power that worketh in us (Ephesians 3:20).*

Believers all over the world should run back to God because without Him, we can do nothing **(John 15:5).** The Bible helps us to understand that the prayers of the righteous availeth much *(James 5:16).*

1

We have been mandated to pray without ceasing *(1 Thessalonians 5:17)*. God is faithful to answer your prayers and give you rest. He is ever attentive to our pleas.

> *Behold, the Lord's hand is not shortened, that it cannot save; neither his ear heavy, that it cannot hear. But your iniquities have separated between you and your God, and your sins have hid his face from you, that He will not hear (Isaiah 59:1-2).*

However, we need to confess our sins and forgive others, which has always been the hindrance to our financial breakthrough and divine healing.

> *But if ye forgive not men their trespasses, neither will your Father forgive your trespasses (Matthew 6:15).*

I have no doubt in my heart that our Heavenly Father will hear your cry as you pray these prayers with faith, and grant you all your heart's desires according to His promises in the name of Jesus.

And this is the confidence that we have in Him, that, if we ask any thing according to his will, He heareth us (1 John 5:14).

Testimonies will abound as you start praying daily to build a relationship with God.

You are blessed and highly favored in the name of Jesus, Amen.

PRAYER OF REPENTANCE AND FORGIVENESS

Dear God, I thank you for your undying love that you have lavished upon my family and I. I appreciate you for your faithfulness and kindness. As I pray the following prayers of financial breakthrough and divine healing, I seek your forgiveness for all knowing and unknowing sins on today. I pray that if I have any unforgiveness in my heart that I am not aware of, I forgive and release it on today. I pray that you cleanse me with your blood and make me holy even as you are holy.

I declare that I become righteous by your mercy, because I have been made the righteousness of God through Christ **(2 Corinthians 5:21**). I declare, henceforth, your spirit comes into my life and directs my path. It is well with my soul. Father, thank you for answering my prayers, Amen

25 POWERFUL PRAYERS FOR FINANCIAL BREAKTHROUGH

FINANCIAL BREAKTHROUGH
PRAYER ONE

Thus saith the Lord, thy Re-
deemer, the Holy One of Israel;
I am the Lord thy God which
teacheth thee to profit, which
leadeth thee by the way that thou
shouldest go (Isaiah 48:17).

Your word is true. The scripture says you honor your word more than your name **(Psalm 138:2).** You are a promise keeping God and with you, all things are possible **(Luke 1:37).**

Your word says,

Behold, I am the Lord, the God
of all flesh: is there anything too
hard for me? (Jeremiah 32:27).

I declare and decree, every impossible situation of my life becomes possible in the name of Jesus. There is nothing too difficult for God to do; therefore, nothing godly shall be impossible for me in Jesus' name.

Jehovah Jireh, teach me to profit in my business and new endeavors in the name of Jesus. Lead me into the path of prosperity. I

decree, I have a plethora of testimonies a-round me. Henceforth, I become unstoppable and unbreakable.

I rebuke every spirit of distraction and error. Today and beyond, I begin to live my life according to the word of God. I begin to engage in right ventures that will boost my finances in accordance with the will of God.

I will not experience poverty anymore. I have every good thing I desire in abundance. I cultivate the habit of giving to the needy. I will not suffer any lack as I give throughout the days of my life.

I believe you have done it and it is well with me in Jesus' name, Amen.

FINANCIAL BREAKTHROUGH PRAYER TWO

For with God nothing shall be impossible (Luke 1:37).

O Lord my God, the creator of heaven and earth, I have come to you today for supernatural financial release.

My financial abundance shall not be impossible. I know you honor your words and keep your promises. You are not a man that you should lie; neither a son of man that you should repent (Numbers 23:19).

Father, honor your promise of abundance in my life today. You promised the children of Israel abundance, and you did it for them with ease. You are a faithful Father, and you have proven this in diverse ways. My trust in you is unshakable and unbreakable because you are a faithful God. Bless me according to your riches in glory by Christ Jesus. Release your financial blessings on me today. I declare abundance into my life, throughout my years in the name of Jesus.

I submit, I am helpless without you. My knowledge and skills cannot sustain me. I request for your abundant grace to prosper in these difficult times. I come to you today through your only begotten Son, Jesus Christ.

Bless my life with abundant finance. I declare, I will not lack anything good. Henceforth, I will live in abundance. Every curse of poverty, lack and debt is destroyed in the name of Jesus, Amen.

FINANCIAL BREAKTHROUGH
PRAYER THREE

"...for it is he that giveth thee power to get wealth..." (Deuteronomy 8:18).

Therefore, I receive power to get wealth. You have power over everything in this world including finance. You breathe the breath of life to everything and you make all things new. Breathe life and grace upon my business ventures and finances.

You have power over every force and principality. Father, regardless of their source, every principality, fueling poverty in my life is totally destroyed today by your fire.

I receive your supernatural blessing for financial release. Lord, by your mercy and power, open your fountain of blessings on me and cause me to prosper in all areas of my life, in Jesus' name.

O Lord, my God, put an end to suffering and lack in my life today.

But my God shall supply all your needs according to his riches in

***glory by Christ Jesus (Phili-
ppians 4:19).***

All my needs are met. My supply exceeds my
demand. Dear Lord, I know you are faithful to
keep your words. Therefore, open doors of
opportunities that will lead me into divine
prosperity in the name of Jesus name.

Today, I declare, I am blessed beyond my
expectations. My family, friends, colleagues,
and everyone around me will call me a blessing. This I pray and receive it through Jesus
Christ our Lord, Amen.

FINANCIAL BREAKTHROUGH PRAYER FOUR

My God, I know there is no impossible case with you. Open every door of prosperity that has been shut against me. By your mercy and love, change my financial status and perfect all that concerns me.

Starting from today, I declare miracles to happen in my life on hourly basis. I declare, everything I lay my hands on shall prosper. My business will flourish in Jesus' name. My family will experience blessings in all ramifications.

> *Beloved, I wish above all things that thou mayest prosper and be in health, even as thy soul prospereth (3 John 2).*

Father, I shall prosper in my health, soul, finances, marriage, career, business and every endeavor of life in Jesus' name. I am a blessing to everyone around me. I shall experience your supernatural financial release in my business and investments and in all facets of my life in the name of Jesus.

Henceforth, I shall excel effortlessly. I shall record success in all areas of my life. My finance receives the touch of God. I shall not borrow but I will lend to nations of the world. Kings and noblemen shall serve me in the name of Jesus. Your mercy shall speak for me in my time of need.

Thank you, Lord, for answering my prayer!

FINANCIAL BREAKTHROUGH PRAYER FIVE

Jesus Christ the same yesterday, and today, and forever (Hebrews 13:8).

My Savior, the creator of all things, I thank you for my inheritance in you. I appreciate you for your love, goodness, and mercy that endures forever.

You are the same yesterday, today and forever. I praise your holy name because I am blessed. I am blessed in all ramifications: family, finance, ministry and endeavors.

Lord, I thank you, because henceforth, lack shall be eternally banished from my life and family. I thank you for changing and promoting my financial status.

Jesus Christ of Nazareth, I know you love me and your thoughts towards me are thoughts of peace to give me an expected end. You know exactly what I need to live a comfortable life.

Though he was rich, yet for your sakes he became poor, that ye through his poverty might be rich (2 Corinthians 8:9).

I decree, I shall not experience poverty anymore in Jesus' name. I will fulfill all His wonderful promises for my life.

Lord, I thank you for your mercy and love upon my life. I give you all the glory, honor and adoration because you have answered my prayer. Blessed be your holy name, Lord Jesus. Amen.

FINANCIAL BREAKTHROUGH PRAYER SIX

And I knew that thou hearest me always: but because of the people which stand by I said it, that they may believe that thou hast sent me (John 11:42).

I bless your Holy name Lord, because you always listen to me whenever I call on you. Jehovah Jireh, I worship you. I exalt your Holy name because you are the only one that can grant my heart's desires. I trust and believe in your providence. Thank You, Lord Jesus.

When men are cast down, then thou shalt say, there is lifting up; and he shall save the humble person (Job 22:29).

I declare lifting up in all I plan to accomplish today. My blessing is not dependent on the economy of this world. I pray for your divine financial release that will distinguish me from unbelievers. Lord, I pray that you make ways for me, where there is no way.

"...and the wilderness be a fruitful field, and the fruitful

field be counted for a forest"
(Isaiah 32:15).

I declare, in the name of Jesus, financial dryness becomes a thing of the past. Father, turn my financial wilderness to a fruitful field, thereby making my fruitful field become a financial forest. I will never run out of supply.

I appreciate your promises and their fulfillment in my finances. I bless your name because success is guaranteed in all areas of my life. I shall endlessly experience and enjoy your abundant financial blessings every day of my life.

It is well with my finances in Jesus' name. I will have a testimony before the end of today.

FINANCIAL BREAKTHROUGH PRAYER SEVEN

Dear Lord, thank you for your daily blessings. I adore your greatness and worship your majesty.

> *And it shall come to pass in that day, that his burden shall be taken away from off thy shoulder, and his yoke from off thy neck, and the yoke shall be destroyed because of the anointing (Isaiah 10:27).*

I declare and decree in the name of Jesus; every yoke of poverty and lack is broken forever in my life. Every burden of debt is lifted from my life. A special anointing for increase and financial breakthrough comes upon me in Jesus' name.

I curse financial disability in my life. I decree, I walk in financial dominion. My financial horns are lifted like that of the unicorn.

> *The Lord is my shepherd; I shall not want (Psalm 23:1).*

Father, I am the sheep of your pasture, therefore, I shall lack no good thing. In the name of Jesus, I declare financial fruitfulness. As the Lord lives, my cup shall overflow with blessings. I declare and decree peace like still waters in my finances. No more uproar and financial tragedy in Jesus' name. My household is favored. My finances are blessed in Jesus' name. Cankerworms are removed from my enterprise totally and forever.

I receive financial blessings in uncountable folds everywhere I turn to. Nations, as well as, people are directed to bless my life in Jesus' name. I shall not lack any good thing. I silence every satanic power that brings financial embarrassment to me. As from today onward, my coast is enlarged in Jesus' name.

Father, I thank you for answering my prayer. Blessed be your Holy Name. Amen.

FINANCIAL BREAKTHROUGH PRAYER EIGHT

Blessed is the man that trusteth in the Lord, and whose hope the Lord is. For he shall be as a tree planted by the waters, and that spreadeth out her roots by the river, and shall not see when heat cometh, but her leaf shall be green; and shall not be careful in the year of drought, neither shall cease from yielding fruit (Jeremiah 17:7-8).

Your words are true and powerful. They reveal your sincere intention towards your children who believe in you. Thank you for making your grace available for me. By your grace, I am saved and I have access to all spiritual blessings.

I am planted by the living water; therefore, my financial connection spreads in the name of Jesus. I shall not experience financial hotness. I shall not stop making profit in my ventures, as my business grow. I receive abundance beyond measure. I command my angels to bring financial breakthrough my way. I receive the grace of ease; I will not struggle to excel in Jesus' name.

Father, every financial door I knock shall open. Regardless of the prevalent economic situation, I will not experience lack. My finances are abundantly blessed. The Lord will make a way for me where there is no way. By your mercy, whatever I lay my hands on shall prosper in Jesus' name.

I bless your name because you are the only true God. Jesus Christ, I thank you for your provision. It is well with my soul. Amen.

FINANCIAL BREAKTHROUGH PRAYER NINE

Blessed be the Lord, who daily loadeth us with benefits, even the God of our salvation (Psalm 68:19).

 My Heavenly Father, I bless you because you daily load me daily with blessings. Blessed be your name in the heavens and on earth. Lord Jesus, the owner of my soul and the one who knows my heart's desires, I have come to you today for your financial release, Father Lord, grant my heart's desires today in Jesus' name.

And God is able to make all grace abound toward you; that ye, always having all sufficiency in all things, may abound to every good work (2 Corinthians 9:8).

I declare and decree, your grace abounds towards me. I operate in the realm of a-bundance and sufficiency. I rebuke poverty and greed. I activate in the grace of more than enough. My overflow of oil shall not dry; my barrel of wheat shall always be full. Empti-

ness of every type is forever gone in Jesus' name.

I have everything I need and plenty leftover to share with others. Not any of my family members will live in poverty any longer. We all delight in the abundance made available by Christ in Jesus' name.

I command supernatural showers of financial blessings to fall on me. I receive the anointing for everlasting financial release in Jesus' name. I do not have any cause to fear because my Father in heaven has settled everything. Jehovah Jireh has made everything new for me. No lack anymore! No poverty anymore! No debt! I am abundantly blessed.

Thank you, Lord, for answering my prayers. Amen

FINANCIAL BREAKTHROUGH PRAYER TEN

The blessing of the Lord, it maketh rich, and he addeth no sorrow with it (Proverbs 10:22).

Your words and promises are just and true. In your name, I pray for riches without sorrow. Everlasting Father, make every crooked way in my life straight. I look unto you and receive help in Jesus' name. I declare indescribable wealth and uncommon riches into my life and family. Your word states,

I will lift up mine eyes unto the hills, from whence cometh my help. My help cometh from the Lord, which made heaven and earth (Psalm 121:1-2).

As the servant looks unto the master, I ask for help from my Father, let there be divine intervention in every matter of my life in Jesus' name. I declare, the earth shall bring its abundance and increase. The wealth of the heathen shall be brought unto me. I shall possess the gates of my enemies.

You created everything and they obey your commands. By Your authority, I command every element to work in my favor, thereby, bringing financial breakthrough. Your word says I shall be the head and not the tail. I will not borrow but lend to nations of the world. By your grace, let this come to pass in my life.

Nothing will work against my financial release. Every hindrance or attack against my prosperity is destroyed. My Heavenly Father is rich. Therefore, I will not lack in Jesus' name. I declare and decree that my cup will not run dry in the mighty name of Jesus.

Henceforth, I shall experience improvement in my finances from today and for the rest of my life. My job, home, family and church is blessed.

I will always sing of your praise, because you have answered my prayers. I thank you, Lord Jesus, Amen.

FINANCIAL BREAKTHROUGH
PRAYER ELEVEN

I bless you Lord for your mercy and goodness. Your word is full of wisdom and knowledge to guide us on how to live our lives according to your will. Glory, honor and adoration be to your name.

> *But seek ye first the kingdom of God, and his righteousness; and all these things shall be added unto you (Matthew 6:33).*

I have sought your kingdom because I have been saved by the blood of Jesus and I am committed to the advancement of the Kingdom. Today, I declare that financial blessings will be made available for me in the name of Jesus. My family, friends, and colleagues shall experience your supernatural touch in all areas of their lives. Every curse of poverty, debt, lack and failure is destroyed over my life.

> *With long life will I satisfy him, and shew him my salvation (Psalm 91:16).*

Today, I claim your prophecies of increase for my life in the name of Jesus. The power of poverty over my life is. Debt and bankruptcy is not my portion. Whoever seeks to demote me in my place of work will experience the wrath of God. I prophesy financial breakthrough into my life today and forevermore. Nothing will hinder me from making progress in the name of Jesus.

> *"No weapon that is formed against thee shall prosper; and every tongue that shall rise against thee in judgment thou shalt condemn. This is the heritage of the servants of the Lord, and their righteousness is of me, saith the Lord" (Isaiah 54:17).*

Henceforth, no evil plan, policy and attempt of the wicked shall prosper against me in Jesus' name. Every tongue speaking loss, retrogression, negativity and financial pain is hereby condemned in the mighty name of Jesus. I declare an immediate turnaround, breakthrough, major miracle, greatness and financial bliss in the name of Jesus.

Thank you, Lord Jesus, for answering my prayer. I love you! Amen.

FINANCIAL BREAKTHROUGH PRAYER TWELVE

And to Jesus the mediator of the new covenant, and to the blood of sprinkling, that speaketh better things than that of Abel (Hebrews 12:24).

My Savior, I fear and honor you. I believe in your work and through your salvation, I have been made whole. I am renewed and made whole by the blood of Jesus.

I prophesy concerning my life that great doors of opportunities are opened unto me. You are Jehovah El Shaddai, the God of more than enough. I declare and decree an overflow of abundance and surplus into my life in the name of Jesus.

My entire family and I live in abundance. Unquantifiable wealth and riches are made available for me because I honor your words and obey your commandments.

And I will make them and the places round about my hill a blessing; and I will cause the shower to come down in his season; there shall be showers of blessing (Ezekiel 34:26).

You made promises of divine shower of blessings in your word. Therefore, I become rich by your blessings upon my life. Nothing will work against my progress. Success is my portion. I shall not sweat before I eat. I bask in the abundant grace of the Most High. By your mercy, I am rich and wealthy.

Who is he that saith, and it cometh to pass, when the Lord commandeth it not? (Lamentations 3:37).

Every negative word uttered against my life shall not stand. My Heavenly Father will satisfy me with amazing gifts that will bring an end to the reign of poverty in my life. It is well with my life. Amen.

FINANCIAL BREAKTHROUGH PRAYER THIRTEEN

Enter into his gates with thanksgiving, and into his courts with praise: be thankful unto Him, and bless his name (Psalm 100:4).

Everlasting Father of the universe, I come into your presence today with joy and thanksgiving in my heart. I declare you as my Father. You are the giver of life and every good thing.

Let them shout for joy, and be glad, that favour my righteous cause: yea, let them say continually, Let the Lord be magnified, which hath pleasure in the prosperity of his servant (Psalm 35:27).

Accept my shout of joy and praise in honor of your unending righteousness. Let your name be magnified in my life O Lord. I believe I am exceedingly blessed today and beyond, because you have pleasure in my prosperity. My prosperity is your desire and that is why I am confident that you will increase my finances and boost my wealth.

I am grateful because you listen to me every time I call upon your name. I prophesy that my day is blessed in the mighty name of Jesus. Everything I lay my hands upon shall prosper.

I rebuke every cankerworm, palmerworm and devourer in my finances. I shall prosper. God will fulfill all his promises for my life.

> *For I know the thoughts that I think toward you, saith the Lord, thoughts of peace, and not of evil, to give you an expected end. (Jeremiah 29:11).*

I receive the manifestation of his thoughts of peace and progress in all areas of my life. I declare every spirit of retrogression and failure become powerless in my life by the power in the name of Jesus. I am blessed and forever lifted in Jesus' name.

FINANCIAL BREAKTHROUGH PRAYER FOURTEEN

I, even I, have spoken; yea, I have called him: I have brought him, and he shall make his way prosperous (Isaiah 48:15).

I receive the power to become prosperous in the name of the Father, the Son, and the Holy Spirit. You have called me into a prosperous way, and I have answered your call. Therefore, I declare an unprecedented prosperity in my life and family. Father, in the name of Jesus, I rebuke and render powerless every orchestration from hell to antagonize my breakthrough.

And I will restore to you the years that the locust hath eaten, the cankerworm, and the caterpiller, and the palmerworm, my great army which I sent among you (Joel 2:25).

Father, I order your host of angels to restore every good thing that I had lost in the past. I declare total restoration of my health, marriage, finances, ministry and gifts that have been stolen away from me by sin in the name of Jesus. The power of sin is rebuked and banished in my life.

> *And thine ears shall hear a word behind thee, saying, this is the way, walk ye in it, when ye turn to the right hand, and when ye turn to the left (Isaiah 30:21).*

Today, I receive divine direction and inspiration to know the right thing to do that will open the door of prosperity for me. I refuse to engage in fruitless. My Heavenly Father will cause people to bless me. I will be highly favored in my place of work. My family, friends and colleagues will join me to praise you for great things you will do in my life. No more loss! No more failures! No more debt! No more financial miscarriages in the mighty name of Jesus.

I thank you Father for redeeming, receiving and blessing me in tremendous manner. Blessed be your Holy name. Amen.

FINANCIAL BREAKTHROUGH
PRAYER FIFTEEN

Thou hast caused men to ride over our heads; we went through fire and through water: but thou broughtest us out into a wealthy place (Psalm 66:12).

As I journey through this year, I receive financial blessings. You Lord, will take me to my wealthy place. I will not have any cause to beg for anything throughout my years on earth. This new year is blessed for my financial success in the name of Jesus. Every aspect of my life shall enjoy your supernatural blessings. You make your elects rich without adding sorrow; therefore, I enjoy unlimited financial provisions made available by my heavenly Father.

I will call on one and thousands shall answer me, because I have been anointed with the oil of prosperity. Nothing will stop me from excelling in all that I do this year in the name of Jesus. This is my year of abundant miracles, amazing success and financial stability. Nothing will ruin my progress.

For sin shall not have dominion over you: for ye are not under the law, but under grace (Romans 6:14).

Sin will no longer have dominion over me. I am holy as my Savior is holy. Henceforth, I curse financial backwardness in the mighty name of Jesus.

My head is lifted like the horn of a unicorn. I declare and decree, I increase in wisdom and knowledge of the Almighty to create wealth. Everything about me is blessed. I move to my promise land without any hindrance.

Glory be to your Holy name. Hallelujah.

FINANCIAL BREAKTHROUGH PRAYER SIXTEEN

Bring ye all the tithes into the storehouse, that there may be meat in mine house, and prove me now herewith, saith the Lord of hosts, if I will not open you the windows of heaven, and pour you out a blessing, that there shall not be room enough to receive it (Malachi 3:10).

My God, I am faithful with my tithes. I obey your commandments. I have been committed to obeying your will as instructed in the scripture. I triumph in your promises because they are just and true. Your word restores peace and makes provision available.

Dear Father, I ask for the enabling grace to walk in the path of righteousness throughout my lifetime. I believe that by having you, I have all things. I decree, I have all things that pertain to life and godliness.

Blessed be your Holy name. You have wealth in abundance, therefore I order great inflow of money into my bank accounts.

By your power Lord, direct riches to my path today and forever.

I receive the giving grace to give to the needy and I receive a good measure, pressed down, and running over in return in the name of Jesus. My heavenly Father, open the floodgates in abundance and cause your rain of blessings to fall on me.

I achieve with ease those things that my mates struggle to accomplish. Nations shall call me blessed, because I am blessed by the Lord in the mighty name of Jesus. In your mighty name, I rebuke wasters and devourers. Every hole the enemies have created in my bag is closed and turns to a source of blessing now by the power in the name of Jesus.

Everlasting Father, I will use my wealth to advance your kingdom. Glory be to your name! Amen.

FINANCIAL BREAKTHROUGH
PRAYER SEVENTEEN

King of glory, I worship your Holy name, for your goodness and mercy that you have bestowed on me. Thank you Father, because it is your grace that has brought me this far. I return all glory, honor and adoration to your name. Blessed be your name in Heaven.

> *So shall thy barns be filled with plenty, and thy presses shall burst out with new wine (Proverbs 3:10).*

O Lord, I declare surplus in my finances in the name of Jesus. I declare, my barn will be filled with plenty and my presses will burst out with new wine. My floors shall be full of wheat and my vats shall overflow with wine and oil. These are your promises, Lord. Speedily bring all your promises of prosperity and financial increase to pass in my life and ministry.

I have known that regardless of the scarcity in the jungle, the lion cannot eat grass. You have placed a greater value on me than the lion. Therefore, no matter what the economy is saying and the prediction of economic analysts, I shall not lack in the name of Jesus. All I want to believe is your word, not the prediction of mortals.

I will shine brighter than the sun this year and beyond. I will not depend on anyone for my needs. Your grace and mercy will sustain me. No matter how difficult things are, the Lord will lift up my head and make me successful.

I am a giver. I refuse to beg for substance. By your power, I overcome every spirit of procrastination that has held me stagnant for a long time.

Blessed be your name, for granting me financial breakthrough.

FINANCIAL BREAKTHROUGH PRAYER EIGHTEEN

The steps of a good man are ordered by the Lord: and he delighteth in his way (Psalm 37:23).

Dear Lord, open my eyes to the right place meant for me to stay and enjoy your supernatural financial release. I am tired of wandering like a sheep without a shepherd. I receive your divine direction to walk in the right path that leads to abundance.

You directed the path of the children of Israel through the wilderness to their promised land, O Lord, direct my path today and forever.

And I am come down to deliver them out of the hand of the Egyptians, and to bring them up out of that land unto a good land and a large, unto a land flowing with milk and honey; unto the place of the Canaanites, and the Hittites, and the Amorites, and the Perizzites, and the Hivites, and the Jebusites (Exodus 3:8).

After the order of the children of Israel, deliver me from all forms of slavery and bring me to the land flowing with milk and honey. You that relocated Israel into the land of plenty, Father, bring me into the realm of abundance and more than enough. Father, do it today and change my financial status by your grace.

> *If any of you lack wisdom, let him ask of God, that giveth to all men liberally, and upbraideth not; and it shall be given him (James 1:5).*

I pray for wisdom to become innovative and creative, obeying the word of God, which will open the floodgates of heaven unto me. No unfavorable policy made by the government or prediction of the evil ones will stop me from flourishing this year in the name of Jesus.

> *"...No good thing will he withhold from them that walk uprightly" (Psalm 84:11).*

No good opportunity will slip off my hands. I receive the grace to convert every opportunity that comes my way to something productive. Failure is not my portion.

When people are complaining of lack, I will rejoice in your name, for the abundance you have granted me. O Lord, bless my way. Thank you, Father.

FINANCIAL BREAKTHROUGH PRAYER NINETEEN

Dear Lord, I bless you for the gift of life. I appreciate your faithfulness over my life. King of kings and Lord of lords, I exalt and lift you up high.

Lord, I have come once again to your presence; I am in your court to seek your face for abundance. This scripture is filled with amazing promises for those that love the Lord.

> *Riches and honor are with me; yea, durable riches and righteousness (Proverbs 8:18)*

You love and delight in those that love you and follow your precepts. Therefore, I will enjoy all that is contained in your love. I have accepted the life of Christ who suffered and died for my sins on the cross of Calvary.

> *I love them that love me; and those that seek me early shall find me (Proverbs 8:17).*

I bless your name because I have found you. I praise your Holy name Lord, be magnified. I shall enjoy your love as I seek your face.

Riches and honor are with you, Lord; you have durable riches and righteousness in your care. I declare an abundant intake of your riches and honor. You cause those that love you to inherit your substance and fill their treasure. Lord, I identify myself with these promises and I command them to come to fulfillment in my life.

I declare; I am rich, blessed, endowed, empowered and preferred in the name of Jesus. The rain of blessings falls on.

I thank you, Lord, for your goodness. It is well with me in the name of Jesus.

FINANCIAL BREAKTHROUGH
PRAYER TWENTY

Dear Lord, I bless you Father for your love over my life. I thank you because you are always there for me. You have been my present help in the time of need.

> *I come: in the volume of the book it is written of me (Psalm 40:7).*

You know everything about me. My strengths and weaknesses are not hidden from you. You know those things I need as your child. Your eyes are bright enough to search through my heart and see my desires. Glorious Father, all my needs can only be met by you. I come boldly before your presence today for spiritual blessings and financial release. Father, bless me today.

I pray for your abundant grace. Your word makes me understand that your mercy prevails on the throne of judgment. I seek you and your kingdom. I believe in your promises and walk according to your will. I am not being swayed by the wind of events. I am steadfast and focused.

I do not believe in any other god for provision. I do not have hope in anyone except you, my Father.

My faith is anchored on you, O Lord. You are my source, strength, bulwark and sustainer. Take away every form of reproach and shame from my life today in the name of Jesus.

I pray that you bless me abundantly today. Any form of embargo on my way inhibiting me from entering my land that flows with milk and honey is destroyed by your power.

I thank you blessed Father. It is well with my soul in Jesus' name. Amen.

FINANCIAL BREAKTHROUGH
PRAYER TWENTY-ONE

Behold the fowls of the air: for they sow not neither do they reap, nor gather into barns; yet your heavenly Father feedeth them. Are you not much better than they (Matthew 6:26).

Father of creation, I receive my daily bread. Thank you for feeding me with plenty.

And God blessed them, and God said unto them, Be fruitful, and multiply, and replenish the earth, and subdue it: and have dominion over the fish of the sea, and over the fowl of the air, and over every living thing that moveth upon the earth (Genesis 1:28).

I rule and reign in dominion, over every creature and power. I have been made to be better than the fishes of the sea and the birds of the air. If you can provide for them so much that they have in abundance, my provider, I declare and decree abundance and surplus provision in the name of Jesus.

Dear Father, I claim my inheritance in you. In the name of Jesus, I silence every voice that has been polluting my financial breakthrough.

> *I know thy works: behold, I have set before thee an open door, and no man can shut it (Revelation 3:8).*

I command every door of opportunity that has been shut against me to open. Your provision is made available for me in surplus today and for the rest of my life. Every wall of impossibility erected against my finances are disgraced after the order of the wall of Jericho.

I refuse to suffer because you are my Jehovah Jireh. My God is more than able to provide for all my needs according to His riches in glory. I am of the Lord and He will bless me with all spiritual blessings in heavenly places.

I receive it in Jesus' name, Amen.

FINANCIAL BREAKTHROUGH PRAYER TWENTY-TWO

Come unto me, all ye that labour and are heavy laden, and I will give you rest. Take my yoke upon you, and learn of me; for I am meek and lowly in heart: and ye shall find rest unto your souls (Matthew 11:28-29).

Dear Savior, you are the omnipotent God. You know how burdened I am. I request for freedom and rest in Jesus' name. I have come today to receive a life full of peace and prosperity to function more effectively in your sanctuary and to take your light to the Gentiles.

Blessed Father, answer my prayer today in the name of Jesus. Take away lack from my life. Grant unto me your unlimited favor and fill my life with prosperity and abundance.

For ye know the grace of our Lord Jesus Christ, that, though he was rich, yet for your sakes he became poor, that ye through his poverty might be rich (2 Corinthians 8:9).

I declare and decree the emergence of God's riches in my life. I am rich.

Favor shall pursue and overtake me. I trust you because you are not a man that you should lie.

It is well with my soul today. I thank you for blessing me. Amen.

FINANCIAL BREAKTHROUGH
PRAYER TWENTY-THREE

Jehovah Jireh, I worship you today and I appreciate you for your kindness and provision over my life. Your words are true. You are not a man that you should lie, neither a son of man that you should repent. I meditate on your words day and night and I am confident that you will bless my life as promised.

> ***Thus saith the Lord, thy Redeemer, the Holy One of Israel; I am the Lord thy God which teacheth thee to profit, which leadeth thee by the way that thou shouldest go (Isaiah 48:17).***

I will have speedy growth in all my ventures, making great profit in all endeavors. I receive insight into new wealth streams. You Lord, will open my eyes of understanding to discover the best place for me. I declare and decree no more loss or death. For my sake, the roads are sanctified and safe. No more accidents throughout this year in the name of Jesus.

Every financial blessing you have allocated to me will not elude me. Abundant rain of prosperity shall fall on me today and throughout my lifetime.

When people are saying there is casting down, my pleasant condition shall say there is lifting up, because you will fill up my house with good things. My mouth shall be filled with testimonies and new songs.

> *As the mountains are round about Jerusalem, so the Lord is round about his people from henceforth even for ever (Psalm 125:2).*

I declare, my source of income will not be attacked. My finances are shielded by the Lord. I pray for more wisdom, knowledge and understanding to recognize opportunities around me and convert them to prosperity. My stream of income shall not dry. Nothing will hinder my progress henceforth.

Thank You, Lord Jesus. I am blessed forever in the mighty name of Jesus. Amen.

FINANCIAL BREAKTHROUGH
PRAYER TWENTY-FOUR

Dear Jesus, I thank you for saving my life from perdition. Glory be to your Holy name for your amazing grace over my life. I bless your name and return all glory, honor and adoration to you.

Give us this day our daily bread (Matthew 6:11).

Lord, I have come to you today to seek your help over my finances. I pray for an increase in my finances. I pray for your grace to lead me right and direct my path throughout this year. I do not want to languish in poverty anymore. I do not want to suffer before I have my daily bread. Bless me Lord and fill my house with your riches.

"...Ye shall eat the riches of the gentiles, and in their glory shall ye boast yourselves" (Isaiah 61:6).

Father Lord, make me prosper and grant me mercy in your sight and in the sight of men. Command people, those I know and those I do not know, to bless me. I will not wallow in

penury this year. Every aspect of my life shall experience increase. I have more than enough. I am blessed all around. Whatever I lay my hands on shall prosper according to your word.

I receive the anointing for supernatural increase and speed. My home is filled with abundance. I shall not borrow. I receive the grace to lend to nations with ease. I shall not go bankrupt.

My family shall not record any loss in the name of Jesus.

Lord, I thank you for answering my prayer; it is well with my finances. Amen.

FINANCIAL BREAKTHROUGH
PRAYER TWENTY-FIVE

For every beast of the forest is mine, and the cattle upon a thousand hills (Psalm 50:10).

Dear Lord, all riches belong to you. You have the key to unlock doors of prosperity. Through your favor, I become prosperous and exceedingly great. Sweet Jesus, hear my cry today and make it easy for me to become rich by your grace.

Father Lord, surprise me in the name of Jesus. I declare, I shall live in riches and wealth throughout the remaining days of my life. I receive financial blessings to have everything I need as a believer.

"...let now thine ear be attentive to the prayer of thy servant, and to the prayer of thy servants, who desire to fear thy name: and prosper, I pray thee, thy servant this day, and grant him mercy in the sight of this man..." (Nehemiah 1:11).

I am your servant, I declare and receive unprecedented financial breakthrough.

My financial success will not be hindered any-more. Whatever negative words that have been spoken against my finances are rendered worthless today by your power. I walk in your power; I walk in miracles and I live a life of favor today and beyond.

> *And I will give thee the treasures of darkness, and hidden riches of secret places, that thou may-est know that I, the Lord, which call thee by thy name, am the God of Israel (Isaiah 45:3).*

I receive the promised. I gain access to the hidden riches of secret places. Henceforth, my eyes are opened to see all concealed goodness, favor, greatness, prosperity and enlargement.

I give to people in abundance because my barn is full and overflowing. My giving grace has been empowered by the Lord. I shall flourish in every kingdom assignment. I meet the need of fellow children of God because I have more than enough.

I bless your name Jesus. It is well with my soul. Hallelujah.

25 PRAYERS FOR DIVINE HEALING

DIVINE HEALING PRAYER
TWENTY-SIX

Beloved, I wish above all things that thou mayest prosper and be in health, even as thy soul prospereth (3 John 2).

L ord Jesus, I thank you for your love over my life. I bless your Holy name for your promises. Thank you because your promises are yes and Amen.

My health is important to you; hence, I will not ignore what you have labeled important. I declare and decree in your name, I shall prosper in my health in the name of Jesus. Like the eagle, my sight, strength, and mental capacity are strengthened.

For I will restore health unto thee, and I will heal thee of thy wounds, saith the Lord; because they called thee an outcast, saying, This is Zion, whom no man seeketh after (Jeremiah 30:17).

I declare total replacement of poor functioning parts in my body in the name of Jesus. I decree, every type of wound is healed. I enjoy the healing grace of the balm of Gilead. Father

Lord, I order every stranger in my body to disappear in Jesus' name. Infirmities are E-gyptian's plagues, I shall see them no more. I have my health perfectly restored in the mighty name of Jesus.

I receive immediate and total divine healing by your power. Naaman came out of the river of Jordan fresh and renewed, therefore I am leaving here totally restored in Jesus mighty name.

I am the temple of the living God, not the storehouse of infirmities; therefore my body refuses to be the dwelling place for sickness. My body fluid is mixed with the blood of Jesus to perfect my healing. No sickness will have a place in my body.

Father, by your mercy, I am strengthened in the name of Jesus. I live in good health. My health receives the fire of the Holy Ghost. In your name, I bind every power of health failure in my life.

I thank you Lord Jesus for answering my prayer. It is well with me. Amen.

DIVINE HEALING PRAYER
TWENTY-SEVEN

Who his own self-bare our sins in his own body on the tree, that we, being dead to sins, should live unto righteousness: By whose stripes ye were healed (I Peter 2:24).

Dear Father, I am in your presence today, O Lord, grant my heart's desires speedily. You own everything in me and I know it is not part of your plan for my life to be held hostage by sickness. Right now, I declare the release of power and strength into my body. Father Lord, heal me of my sicknesses and restore peace to my soul.

I plead for your mercy to deliver me from every attack against my health. Your word says that my body is the temple of God. O Lord, I rebuke every form of attack against your temple. Heal me totally.

Through the death and resurrection of Christ, I confess that my health receives the perfect and divine healing of God. My body will not accommodate infirmity. I receive the grace to live in peace and sound health.

I will not die prematurely. I shall live, I shall not die. Jesus said, "It is finished", I declare, sickness is over, pain is finished and my health is totally restored. The grace of God is sufficient for me in the mighty name of Jesus.

I bless you Father of grace, for your love over my life. I appreciate you for answering my prayer. Glory be to your name!

DIVINE HEALING PRAYER
TWENTY-EIGHT

My Father in heaven, glory be to your Holy name, and I thank you because you are always there for me in any situation.

> *But they that wait upon the Lord shall renew their strength; they shall mount up with wings as eagles; they shall run, and not be weary; and they shall walk, and not faint (Isaiah 40:31).*

As I wait on you, I declare total renewal of my cells, tissues, organs, systems and body parts in Jesus' name. Henceforth, none of my body parts shall be fail, frail, faint or fall off. As I grow in years, my strength shall not dwindle. I tap into the grace of Moses, Joshua, Caleb and other empowered patriarchs. My strength is daily renewed.

> *Ask, and it shall be given you; seek, and ye shall find; knock, and it shall be opened unto you (Matthew 7:7).*

I ask and receive perfect healing, I seek and find restoration, I knock and the door of bodily renewal is opened unto me. Today, grant me quick recovery from my infirmity in the precious name of Jesus.

> **Wherefore God also hath highly exalted him, and given him a name which is above every name. That at the name of Jesus every knee should bow, of things in heaven, and things in earth, and things under the earth (Philippians 2:9-10).**

There is healing and miracles in your name. I command every knee of sickness and infirmity to bow in the name of Jesus. I decree, every force and power strengthening infirmity in my body to be put into bondage in the name of Jesus. I break the chain of health instability.

Everlasting Father, put an eternal end to every assignment of the wicked in my life. I decree, I will not fall sick again. I receive the strength to function effectively in your sanctuary.

Blessed Jesus, I thank you. Let your Holy name be glorified. Amen

DIVINE HEALING PRAYER
TWENTY-NINE

Father Lord, I thank you for enabling me to see the light of today. I adore your Holy name because there is none like you.

> *"...let the weak say, I am strong" (Joel 3:10).*

I receive the reality of God's word. My health is strong, my mental capacity is strong, and my weakness is totally turned into strength in Jesus' name. Today, I boldly come to your presence with expectations and I strongly believe I will not be disappointed. Heavenly Father, heal me completely today. I declare, my health challenges are terminated.

> *He healeth the broken in heart, and bindeth up their wounds (Psalm 147:3).*

I pray for divine healing in the name of Jesus. Nothing will work against my health anymore. Whatever is plaguing my health with evil is destroyed by fire in the mighty name of Jesus. My wounds are healed and my broken heart is comforted.

*He sent his word, and healed
them, and delivered them from
their destructions
(Psalm 107:20).*

I receive the sent word; therefore, I am healed.
Father Lord, today, send your angels of
healing to my life. Your suffering, death, bu-
rial and resurrection have perfected my health
concerns; therefore, I declare and decree, sickness is not my portion in Jesus' name.

*Blotting out the handwriting of
ordinances that was against us,
which was contrary to us, and
took it out of the way, nailing it
to his cross (Colossians 2:14).*

Every evil pronouncement against my health
is nullified. I command every arrow of death
shot against my life to backfire.

I thank you Lord, for answering my prayer. It
is well with my soul in Jesus' name. Amen.

DIVINE HEALING PRAYER
THIRTY

Everlasting King of Glory, I praise you for the wonderful promises you have made for my health. I believe you because I am healed already at the mention of your name. I thank you Jesus.

> *Confess your faults one to another, and pray one for another, that ye may be healed. The effectual fervent prayer of a righteous man availeth much. (James 5:16).*

Heavenly father, forgive any sin in me that has allowed sickness to enter into my life. I confess my inadequacies and iniquities, Lord, heal me now. I reject any company that may lure me into sin and I pray that you strengthen me to keep your commandments and walk according to your precepts.

Jehovah Rapha, I pray that affliction will not rise a second time in the name of Jesus. The wall of Jericho that has fallen will not stand again. My healing shall be permanent. Anyone that may want to resuscitate infirmity in my life shall be silenced forever.

I live in good health and sound mind. My bones, tissues, blood and water shall receive the healing of the Almighty God. No weapon formed against my health shall prosper. I destroy the spirit of infirmity by the blood of the Lamb and by the word of my testimony. Amen.

DIVINE HEALING PRAYER
THIRTY-ONE

Then they cried unto the Lord in their trouble, and he saveth them out of their distresses. He sent his word, and healed them, and delivered them from their destructions. (Psalm 107:19-20).

Jehovah Rapha, I thank you for your word of healing and miracles. I bless your holy name for every good promise you have made in the Scripture. I believe strongly in your power of healing as revealed in the Bible. You are the same yesterday, today and forever.

Lord, heal me totally today and deliver me from sickness, pain and worries in the name of Jesus. Jehovah Rapha, strengthen me and make me whole today. I receive the strength and grace to function effectively in your sanctuary in the mighty name of Jesus.

Every sickness that wants to send me into an early grave is destroyed by your power. Your word sets me free and I am free indeed from every trouble.

I will not waste my fortune on procuring drugs because the blood is more potent than any known drug. Jesus has made me free, whosoever the son has set free is free indeed. I declare, I am totally free in the name of the Father, Son, and the Holy Spirit.

DIVINE HEALING PRAYER
THIRTY-TWO

Heal me, O Lord and I will be healed; save me, and I will be saved: for thou art my praise. (Jeremiah 17:14).

Dear Lord, my healing has been perfected by you. You have shed your blood to perfect my health. Medical Science is limited, but you are the unlimited God. Physicians can only care, but you cure; they are prone to making mistakes, but you are a perfect God.

Lord Jesus, put an end to suffering, pain, disease and sickness in my body in the name of Jesus.

Every source of pain in my life is totally destroyed by the fire of God. I have received the anointing from my heavenly Father to resist every form of attack against my health. The blood of Jesus will purify me and wash away every harmful substance in my body in the mighty name of Jesus. I will not die untimely.

My eyes have seen the beginning of the year and it will end successfully. I will not lose any part of my body to sickness or disease.

Thank you Lord for what you have done. Be thou exalted in Jesus' name.

DIVINE HEALING PRAYER
THIRTY-THREE

O Lord my God, I cried unto thee, and thou hast healed me (Psalm 30:2).

My healer, I bless you for the wondrous things you have done in my life. I lift your name higher than any other name.

Everlasting King of Glory, I pray for your divine healing over my health, and I believe I have been healed. Lord, search through all the parts of my body and uproot every seed of infirmity, pain, sickness and disease in the mighty name of Jesus. The Prince of Peace, supply peace to my life in abundance.

I am too fortified by God to be admitted in any hospital of the world. My body is too protected to be afflicted by sickness. Therefore, I command sickness to vacate my body right now. I speak against every spirit of infirmity. Your time is over, be destroyed by the fire of Holy Ghost.

From henceforth let no man trouble me: for I bear in my bo-

dy the marks of the Lord Jesus (Galatians 6:17).

Henceforth, there shall be a Passover. Sickness and its destructive accomplices shall see me and passover my family and I in the name of Jesus. I carry the mark of exemption; I am exempted from being a victim of evil. From the top of my head to the sole of my feet, I declare perfect healing. Nothing shall work against my health. I am free from the grip and bondage of illness that want to tame me. Your words are unbreakable. I love you sweet Jesus! Amen.

DIVINE HEALING PRAYER
THIRTY-FOUR

And whatsoever ye do in word or deed, do all in the name of the Lord Jesus, giving thanks to God and the Father by him (Colossians 3:17).

Dear Jesus, my body glorifies the name of the most high. I am no longer prone to any attack of the enemy.

Father Lord, I command every pain and infirmity in my life to disappear. I decree, by the power in the name of Jesus, that sickness has no place in my life.

Thou shalt also decree a thing, and it shall be established unto thee: and the light shall shine upon thy ways (Job 22:28).

Father, I decree healing and life, soundness of mind and mental wholeness, strength and bodily health, spiritual and emotional wellness. I am a child of God and I have been given the authority by my Father.

I bind and cast out every spirit of cancer that would try to live in my body. Prostate cancer, Colon cancer, Leukemia, Lung cancer, Bladder cancer, Breast cancer, Cervical cancer, Brain cancer, Liver cancer, Kidney cancer, Bone cancer, Esophageal cancer, Gastric cancer, Endometrial cancer and other forms of cancer, regardless of its names, you are forbidden in my body.

Nothing shall hinder my body, soul and spirit from flourishing. I receive the strength of God to possess good health throughout the days of my life. Any arrow of sadness shot into my life backfires. I have good health to enjoy all the riches and wealth you have given to me. I will not suffer from pain anymore.

I adore you for answering my prayers. Glory be to your Holy name. Amen.

DIVINE HEALING PRAYER
THIRTY-FIVE

But he answered and said, Every plant, which my heavenly Father hath not planted, shall be rooted up (Matthew 15:13).

Father Lord, I bless you for your faithfulness. I thank you because it is your will and expectation that I live in prosperity with good health and a sound mind. I appreciate you Lord for your good thoughts towards me. I know you are not happy with any deviation in my state of health. You want me to be strong, agile and fit to bring the reality of your gospel to the people in the world.

Blessed Jesus, I enter into your Holy court and ask for total restoration of my health. Lord, sickness is not part of the redemption package you promised me; therefore, I dislodge every reality that is different from your plan. Your plan is that I live long in good health to proclaim your good works in the land of the living.

Today, I command every evil plantation to be uprooted in the mighty name of Jesus. Sickness is an evil plant; therefore, I command the

spirit of sickness and pain to vacate my life right now in the name of Jesus. I command the Holy Ghost to terminate every activity of the wicked ones in my life.

I shall live in good health, prosperity and peace. Amen.

DIVINE HEALING PRAYER
THIRTY-SIX

*I will say of the Lord, He is my
refuge and my fortress: my God;
in him will I trust (Psalm 91:2).*

Dear Lord, I worship you today because you are a miracle worker and a promise keeper that do marvelous things.

I come to your presence today with a burning desire to be healed of my diseases. Father Lord, grant me a speedy recovery from sickness in the name of Jesus.

My body is not the temple of sickness; therefore, I declare every work of the wicked against my health to be wasted by the fire of God. In Jesus' name, I destroy the strongholds of diseases and infirmities.

I will live the remaining days of my life on earth in good health. It shall be well with me. Blessed be your Holy name. Be thou exalted O Lord. I am healed. Amen.

DIVINE HEALING PRAYER
THIRTY-SEVEN

Confess your faults one to another, and pray one for another, that ye may be healed. The effectual fervent prayer of a righteous man availeth much. (James 5:16).

Thank you, Lord Jesus, because I am saved by your grace. I bless you for your mercy over my life. Be thou exalted O Lord.

King of Kings and Jehovah Rapha, I come today to seek your forgiveness; heal me by your mercy. The Bible makes me to understand that your mercy prevails over judgment. Righteous Father, all I seek and desire today is that you release your anointing of divine healing on me, as I exercise my faith in your word.

He sent his word, and healed them, and delivered them from their destructions (Psalm 107:20).

I declare the establishment of these promises in my life and family in the name of Jesus.

Today, I release your word of healing and permanent victory over sin.

I overcome sickness and death by the power of resurrection. I will not have any cause to be admitted in the hospital throughout this year.

Blessed be your name because I am more than a conqueror. I am an overcomer. Amen.

DIVINE HEALING PRAYER
THIRTY-EIGHT

*And he said unto her, Daughter,
thy faith hath made thee whole,
go in peace, and be whole of
your plague. (Mark 5:34).*

Dear Father, I am here today in your presence with my faith rekindled in you. I
remove every form of doubt from my heart
today and I hold on to your promises because
they are just and timely.

I declare total healing for me and my family in
the name of Jesus. We need your strength to
go on with our daily activities without any
hindrance. I know your thoughts toward me
are thoughts of peace and not of evil to give
me an expected end. Therefore, Father, I pray
that you will bless my health today and heal
me from every disease. I wash myself in the
atoning blood of the lamb and command
healing to my bones and tissues. I will not
lose any parts of my body in the name of
Jesus.

Every plague that has been sent into my life is
destroyed by the fire of the Holy Ghost. I
declare peace and good health in my family

throughout this year. No life will be lost. We started this year with our hearts full of joy, and we shall equally end it with joy. The Lord will not put me to shame. I remain in the sanctuary of the almighty where there is peace and safety.

Thank you Lord Jesus. Amen.

DIVINE HEALING PRAYER
THIRTY-NINE

"The Spirit of the Lord is upon me, because he hath anointed me to preach the gospel to the poor, he hath sent me to heal the brokenhearted, to preach deliverance to the captives, and recovering of sight to the blind, to set at liberty them that are bruised," (Luke 4:18).

Dear Lord, thank you for your words of hope and relief. I know those words are not just there to make me happy but they are deliberately written to convey your thoughts to your children.

I am your child, Lord. And I am here today, Lord, meet me at the point of my need. My strength has failed me. My knowledge has not been able to provide the best solutions I need but I look unto you today for my help. Father, bless my health. Dear Father, you are the greatest physician in both the heaven and the earth. Therefore, perfect my healing today in the name of Jesus.

I enjoy good health and sound mind today. I have been delivered from the grip of sickness. Strength has been restored to my body and I begin to do things I couldn't do before. I have been totally healed by Jehovah Rapha.

Thank, you Lord Jesus for quickening my body. I am strong and nothing shall bring me down again in the name of Jesus.

DIVINE HEALING PRAYER
FORTY

"But when Jesus knew it, he withdrew himself from thence: and great multitude followed him, and he healed them all;" (Matthew 12:15).

Dear Lord, prove your power of healing in my life today. I know you are the greatest healer, heal me totally Lord. Your healing is sure and permanent, the type that no man can give. You are the God of all flesh and nothing is impossible for you to do. Blessed Jesus, touch me with your hand of healing at the exact part where I need your touch.

And Jesus went forth, and saw a great multitude, and was moved with compassion toward them, and he healed their sick (Matthew 14:14).

Father, have mercy on me today and relieve me from any pain I am experiencing. Break every curse of infirmity in my life in the name of Jesus. Jesus Christ of Nazareth, I declare my rising from the sickbed today without any delay.

 Thank you, Lord. I believe my healing is certain in the name of Jesus. I shall not feel pain anymore. I bless you Lord for my healing. I thank you Father because I can now walk about doing your work without any hindrance. I will no longer be oppressed by the devil again. I take advantage of the power of God that is present to heal me.

I thank you Jesus, for perfecting my healing. I believe it is well with me in the name of the Father, the Son and the Holy Spirit.

DIVINE HEALING PRAYER
FORTY-ONE

And when the men of that place had knowledge of him, they sent out into all that country round about, and brought unto him all that were diseased; And besought him that they might only touch the hem of his garment: and as many as touched were made perfectly whole. (Matthew 14:35-36).

Sweet Jesus, I have read many true accounts of how you raised the dead and healed the sick in the Bible, and I believe you can do the same in my life. You are the same yesterday, today and forever more.

The greatest healer, I return all glory and adoration unto you and I pray for my healing today. Father Lord, by faith, I receive my perfect healing. My healing is permanent in your name.

Lord, I thank you because you will expurgate every form of disease or infirmity from my life today by your power. I command every spirit of weakness and agony to depart from

my life. Every disease, either known or unknown is destroyed by the power of God. It is well with me in Jesus' name. Grace is made available for me in abundance. I live in good health. No medical challenges anymore.

I have the strength to serve you even more. Blessed be your Holy name. Amen.

DIVINE HEALING PRAYER
FORTY-TWO

And Jesus went about all Galilee, teaching in their synagogues, and preaching the gospel of the kingdom, and healing all manner of sickness and all manner of disease among the people. (Matthew 4:23).

Dear Lord, I know your healing power is real to restore my health. You are a merciful Father who is always interested in seeing your children in good health. Father, I accept you as my Lord and personal Savior and I claim all the promises made to the children of God. I confess it is well with my health.

I decree, no demon will inflict pain on me anymore. I am saved through the death and resurrection of Jesus Christ and I shall no longer be tamed by sickness. Every wall of sickness is broken and I am healed totally. As you healed all manner of sicknesses and diseases, I present myself for permanent healing and I also receive the power to heal the sick in the name of Jesus.

Your word says, "The name of the Lord is a strong tower, the righteous run into it and they are saved." I am righteous by the righteousness of Christ and I claim my right from your healing grace today.

I thank you Jesus for healing me. Hallelujah.

DIVINE HEALING PRAYER
FORTY-THREE

Dear Lord, I have faith that you can heal me and that is why I have come to you this day. You have demonstrated this in countless ways. Precious Father, perfect my healing today by your grace. You only spoke a word to heal the servant of the centurion; I receive your sent word of healing and there-fore declare that I am healed.

Father Lord, heal all my diseases and bring me peace by your name. I declare that my healing happens now in the name of Jesus. I believe your word will heal me totally today.

The Maker of the universe, there is nothing impossible for you to do. Destroy every work of wickedness in my life. Give me the strength to go on with your work. I really want to serve, and take the gospel of Christ to all parts of the world.

I declare and confess that sickness will not hold me back from doing your work. Your grace will sustain me in these tough times. I shall not die but live to preach your good works all over the world.

People will come to see your light through my life in the name of Jesus. Amen!

DIVINE HEALING PRAYER
FORTY-FOUR

Therefore, I say unto you, what things so ever ye desire, when ye pray, believe that ye receive them, and ye shall have them (Mark 11:24).

Dear Savior, I believe I am healed today in the name of Jesus. I believe I have been loosed from the chain of sickness. I believe that I now have my health restored to me. After the order of the woman with the issue of blood, my faith has touched you; heal me completely in Jesus' name.

I remove every spirit of doubt from my heart by the blood of Jesus. I allow the spirit of God to take control of my life. Nothing will work against my healing.

By your grace, I overcome the power of sickness in my life. My body is the temple of God and it shall not be desecrated by infirmity and pain in the mighty name of Jesus. Healing is made available for me today.

I will not struggle to get my healing because Jesus has already paid the price.

I bless you because you are in charge of my life and you will never allow the kingdom of hell to prevail over my health in the name of Jesus. I am blessed in Jesus' name. Amen.

DIVINE HEALING PRAYER
FORTY-FIVE

And his name through faith in his name hath made this man strong, whom ye see and know: yea, the faith which is by him hath given him this perfect soundness in the presence of you all (Acts 3:16).

Dear Lord, I declare miraculous healing that will surprise everyone around me in the name of Jesus. I thirst for your healing today, satisfy me early O Lord that my joy may become full. Father, make your healing power available for me so that I can start doing things I couldn't do before.

Sweet Jesus, I ask for your power to strengthen me and quicken my body. I declare peace and good health concerning myself. I shall not have any cause to run into debt due to my health. My health shall not become a liability for my family.

I speak against every form of disability in my life. I receive the strength of the Almighty to function adequately in your sanctuary.

Every cause of constant fatigue or weakness is destroyed in my life today. I will not have any cause to waste my fortune on health care cost in the name of Jesus. I receive grace to easily adapt to change in weather. As Jesus rebuked the contrary wind, I declare, the atmospheric condition shall not work against my health. I am strong like God throughout the year in the name of Jesus.

I thank you Lord, for answering my prayer. Blessed be your holy name. It is well with my soul in Jesus' name.

DIVINE HEALING PRAYER
FORTY-SIX

And whatever we ask, we receive of him, because we keep his commandments, and do those things that are pleasing in his sight. (I John 3:22).

Dear Father, thank you for your assurance of good health and abundance for my life. You are the greatest healer who heals without collecting a dime. You are more than able to restore my health.

I know one of the causes of sickness and disease is unfaithfulness and refusal to keep your commandments. Father Lord, today I receive the grace to obey your commandments and walk in the path of righteousness. I stop acting contrary to your will in the name of Jesus.

Every sin in me that has precipitated infirmity, Father, I kindly ask for mercy and forgiveness. Father, mend our broken line of communication today. I want to reconnect with you. I have come to realize that only you can solve my problems.

Dear Lord, I request you come to my aid and release your divine healing power and miraclees in my life in Jesus' name.

I thank you Lord for your love. Glory be to your Holy name. Hallelujah.

DIVINE HEALING PRAYER
FORTY-SEVEN

And said, if thou wilt diligently hearken to the voice of the Lord thy God, and give ear to his commandment, keep all his statutes, I will put none of these diseases upon thee, which I have brought upon the Egyptians: for I am the Lord that healeth thee. (Exodus 15:26).

O God, today, I receive an obedient heart, thereby, keeping all your commandments all my years. I pray and receive the grace to serve you with all my heart in the mighty name of Jesus. I declare, I am obedient. Your grace shall be sufficient for me. Only shouts of joy shall be heard in my house. Disease and its accompanying woes are forever banished.

I confess, I am healed in the name of Jesus. I am immune against any diseases by the blood of the lamb. By your grace, I am delivered and healed by your power. Your grace is sufficient for me and I will not abuse it.

I will always be an obedient child. The grace to follow you without falling into sin is re-

leased upon me and I am saved by your grace. Amen.

DIVINE HEALING PRAYER
FORTY-EIGHT

And when he had called unto him his twelve disciples, he gave them power against all unclean spirits, to cast them out, and also to heal all manner of sickness and all manner of diseases (Matthew 10:1).

Dear Savior, I declare the manifestations that follows children of God in my life in the name of Jesus. Father, I receive the power to heal those that are oppressed by the devil. I tap into your power of healing and I am empowered to heal the sick and raise the dead in the name of Jesus. I am filled with the Holy Spirit.

The Grace of God is sufficient for me and I am blessed of the Lord in the name of the Father, the Son and the Holy Spirit.

DIVINE HEALING PRAYER
FORTY-NINE

And God wrought special miracles by the hands of Paul (Acts 19:11).

Father Lord, here I am, do special miracles by my hands in the name of Jesus. I want you to deposit your power of healing into my life, Father Lord, do it in the name of Jesus.

My family is healed. Sickness will not come close to my spouse and children. The power of God is made available to heal all manner of sicknesses and diseases by my hands.

I will not struggle to call on the name of Jesus. Whenever I call on you Jehovah Rapha, you answered me speedily. Impediments are removed from my path. I receive the power to overcome every temptation that the devil may bring my way. I will not fall, faint nor falter in the name of Jesus. I am strong in the Lord. Sickness has no place in my life and in my family.

Father, I thank you, for perfecting my healing and people around me. We live in peace today and every day. In Jesus' name, Amen.

DIVINE HEALING PRAYER
FIFTY

Blessed be the God and Father of our Lord Jesus Christ, who hath blessed us with all spiritual blessings in heavenly places in Christ (Ephesians1:3).

My gracious Father, I thank you Lord for answering all my prayers. I believe my faith in you has made me whole. I have no fear in my heart because I have run into your strong tower. I am assured of your safety. Blessed be your Holy name. I confess that I shall live in good health today and every day.

I declare, no force is permitted to harm me anymore. I receive the grace of the Lord to function adequately and effectively in God's vineyard. Every power that wants to work against my health is destroyed in the name of Jesus.

Your name is higher than any other name. I call on your name today, Father, direct my path and protect me from all manner of sicknesses and diseases. I will not fall sick throughout this year. My family is covered by the blood of Jesus.

He sent his word, and healed them, and delivered them from their destructions (Psalm 107:20).

I declare healing in my life by your power.

It is well with me in the name of the Father, the Son and the Holy Spirit. Blessed be your Holy name.

NOTES

Made in the USA
Middletown, DE
14 April 2022